Stations
of
The Air

JOHN CIARDI

A SLEEP
(BY ROUSSEAU)

The deer stand black by water, the lion's head
comes golden from its cave, the snake goes down
like a brook through ferns. A man who may be dead
lies face up in the puddle of the moon.

Night is the dream about him. Burning birds
brush the breasts of cloud, their colors gone
to black and gold. The trees come down like herds
to drink beside his sleep. Later the lion

Sniffs him and leaves, the deer go trembling by,
the snake spills past. Out of a cloud, Orion
opens and closes on a chalky sky.
The trees fall back and back into the dawn.

—John Ciardi

BkMk Press

1993   University of Missouri-Kansas City

JOHN CIARDI

Stations of The Air

— Thirty-three poems —

Selected and arranged by Miller Williams
Design & type / Michael Annis   Calligraphy / David Ashley
Jacket Art / Michael Bergt

STATIONS OF THE AIR

Poems copyright © 1993 by the Estate of John and Judith Ciardi
ALL RIGHTS RESERVED.

Dust cover art © 1993 by Michael Bergt
Calligraphy © 1993 by David Ashley
Art Direction, Design & Typography by Michael Annis

LIBRARY OF CONGRESS
Library of Congress Cataloging-in-Publication Data

Ciardi, John, 1916-1986.
    Stations of the air : poems / by John Ciardi
      p.   cm.
    ISBN 0-933532-86-5 : $10.50 cloth
    I. Title
PS3505.I27S7   1993
    811'.52—dc20   92-8657
                                                                   CIP

BkMk Press

Dan Jaffe, Director
Rae Furnish, Associate Editor

Except for "Remote Control," the poems included in this collection were discovered among the papers left by John Ciardi at the time of his death on Easter Sunday, 1986. "One Betty—Five Skulls," "Return," and "Visibility Zero" were among those found in a journal published by The University of Arkansas Press as *Saipan: The War Diary of John Ciardi.* "Remote Control" appeared in *The Southern California Anthology,* a publication of the University of Southern California's Master of Professional Writing Program.
"The Logician's Nocturne" appeared in *New Letters,* University of Missouri-Kansas City.

iii	*Frontis*
11	CONTRACT
12	AND THY MOTHER
14	ONE BIRD SONG MORNING STARTED
16	STORM
17	AVERAGES
18	THAT SUMMER SEA
20	A WALK DOWN A MOUNTAINSIDE
21	IF I COULD TELL YOU WHAT I HAVE LOVED HERE
23	SHORE
25	A SLEEP (by Rousseau)
26	FOOD NOTES
28	THIS MORNING
32	AN OLD MAN CONFESSES
34	AN ELEGY FOR MORAL SELF-ASSURANCE AND COUNTRY VIRTUE
36	THE LOGICIAN'S NOCTURNE
37	LOVING YOU IS SOMETHING TO DO
38	CALL IT A DAY

LINES FOR MYRA TO GROW ON	40
CARVING THE TURKEY	41
MAYFLIES	43
ONE BETTY—FIVE SKULLS	46
RETURN	48
VISIBILITY ZERO	49
MR. & MRS.	51
SAINTHOOD	52
THE HERO	53
STATEMENT	54
THE ILLUSIONIST	55
THE RITE	56
REMOTE CONTROL	57
A GRAY SPRING MORNING	58
LAST RITES	60
About the Author	62
Notes on the Artists	63
Contributors	64

CONTRACT

I read to p. 15 and chucked the book.
Not everything's to finish.   It's my turn now
to try to keep you reading.   Have a look.
Mind is what makes itself up.   If somehow
I coax it one page further and one more,
you owe me for your pleasure.   Not before.

And Thy Mother

In my first dark before the world began
God said: "John, John, nothing but tears are true.
Kneel, beat your breast and weep to be a man.
I have your father and I'm watching you."

My mother, deviled soul, wept on His side.
And I, who found myself with three to please,
Lowered my head and beat my breast and cried
To be God's pink-eyed sheep with calloused knees.

Let sons honor their mothers.   Mine was mad
as a Sicilian passion.   Wolf and lamb,
she ripped with her own teeth what flesh she had
and fed it, poisoned, to her young.   I am

The son of deaths to honor.   She meant well,
and died for that—for God, her man, and me.
I housed her death in my first tear that fell
Sweetly for someone else.   Then, washed and free,

I smiled and the world began.   What a long ease
Follows forgiving!   What *was* that dark about?
Those voices?—I can listen long as trees
And nothing happens but the world whirled out.

One Bird Song Morning Started

I thought of singing.   That was no night song.
A sparrow can go lighter to the air
than Plato to music.   Being a man and wrong
and tuneless in my reasons, shall I care
what theorem sets a bird to what it is?
This morning's trees are full of idiocies

that twitter deeper than ten schools of thought.
Could passion doodle sounds, this air's the pad
for every scroll and curlicue and blot
a hand makes when the mind's away.   I had
this daydream from no mind when I was small.
Whose hand did this?   Or was it no hand at all

but bird tracks on a page? I think I knew
the world describes itself in what it is.
I'm learning back: whatever is, is true.
I don't know how to sing it: I'm thinking this,
and therefore losing it. It just won't stay
where thinking puts it. It has all this day

to answer to, get started, and become,
not knowing what comes next. The egg is stocked
with instants only, each itself. No theorem
can count such fractions whole: the mind is locked
to mind and has no key into this day
some hand, or none, scrawls when the mind's away.

Storm

The morning after moonsnow, the bone dunes,
like a mathematician's imagination strewn,
lay saltdead in the sun; their worldless crescents
an invasion of ultimate functions; not sent —
a man could swear to that at a glance — but blown
from the unresembling sense of a last unknown.

Then bit by bit as the sun waxed back toward man —
toward what we think the world is — one by one
that many-faced enforcement of anarchy
began to sweat.   It was possible to see
the ultimate changing back to continuum.
It was possible to think of being at home

on whatever world it is.   It was possible
to think in similes that would do, or all
but do.   So a snow face at the window
began to look like an apple broken in two,
the tears of juice clinging to the quartz flakes
of the split halves, that being how apples break.

And how the impossible mends — which is to say,
how it grows back to resemblance in a day.

Averages

On annual average, about a thousand pink
porcelain cups open on the display rack
of the magnolia by the patio, where I drink
my morning coffee, a guilt across my back

days it's too cold.   Sooner shiver a week
than miss the light that tree pours.   I sleep late
hoping I will have warmed.   It doesn't work.
Not this year.   But cold springs exfoliate

even through dusts of snow.   The faithful go
top-coated, gloved, and shawled, to Easter.   I
sit cold to its first tree and let the glow
perfect me briefly.   A tot of Irish rye
makes up the difference.   After which I shower
in radiant water, baptized by a power.

That Summer Sea

Wading a summer edge, a naked love
dabs a toe in the infinite, splashes back,
and we lie easy, one with the huff and shove,
ourselves a puddle of sea in a skin sack
and thoughtful in reprieve, both seas asprawl.
But who can even think to think it all?

We dawdle by a soft machine of seamless
self-mending rips and jostling hills.   Off shore,
it is a grinder.   Deeper, by sun- and moon-stress,
a tidal heap.   Deepest, a night crush more
than stone, yet ever parting to let down,
like a black mercury, into the billion-ton

last inch of itself, all that had once stood light
and froth-laced in the come-on flounce
of shoulders glistening in the scarved bight.
But dress in all of it and every ounce
becomes a gravity.   Only the skin stays loose;
redundant, palindromic, superfluous.

An acid, it eats everything but gold.
It boils off vapors and then sucks them back
in swirling slurps till, churning hot and cold
it spins the hurricane down its howling track.
Inland a thousand miles it tolls a bell
out of its tower, reforming church and chancel,

till rage is God, and god an interval
in the maul of power that seems to have a cause
but not a reason.   One could fill a pail
and wash the scuppers down in any pause
of demonstration, but all tidiness
drains back into original excess.

For nothing taken for it is itself,
nor itself less.   From the last leadfoot deep
to its slipshod frothing on the coastal shelf
it is the sum more than all parts, a sleep
of spinning particles engrossed beyond
all bells it breaks, all tenure, and all bond.

A Walk Down a Mountainside

By pothole water down a seam of time
   I walked away from Tuesday.   Through my mind
a flap of crows tore from the roof of pine
   like tarpaper from a shack in a high wind.

A blue hole in a green flame, like a lens,
   picked out a cloud.   I stood and watched a drift
out of all focus.   Like a secret sense,
   a squirrel jangled in the nervous lift

of the leaf-net that something wrong was there.
   A blue-jay squawked, "It's true!" and blurred away.
That was the last sound but the water's lain
   long rush through time — a holding silver-gray

and quartz-lit sough, like silence drawing breath
   in the age between two stars.   Locked out, alone,
and with nothing to listen to but the nothing said
   by water going, I threw in a stone

the size of a brain to make one deliberate sound
   of one weighed thing in the anchorless drift.   And restored
to my own humor and gravity, I walked out
   from time to Tuesday, satisfied and ignored.

If I Could Tell You
What I Have Loved Here

If I could tell you what I have loved here
since god-sweated and devil-pinched
men of East Anglia took this land
soon to principle that outran them
and came back larger than they,
magnified by a Jeffersonian rhetoric,
ordained in the blood of The Wilderness,
and burned, branded into the unfreed slave —

if I could tell you, or tell myself
of the lodges faded from the jagged shadow
of the Tetons when the Anglo Saxon,
reverted to barbarism, locked knives,
sweat to sweat on the trails of the reddened snow,
animal and an animalizer of primitives,
and of god, too, till his homestead tamed him
not to a civilization, but to a faith
in the propriety of his prejudice —

and yet in love with his land, with the hills
and flats he could not hold his sons
and daughters to once the cities
had sent their trains.   I could say
we have been mad in Paradise

for all we have been given.   The north rock
of Maine's edge where a man could stand
churched if he would, not necessarily
in God, but in his own first of things,
the Susquehanna flowing from mist
like the gathering of an unknown blessing.

SHORE

In withered summer on a rock,
    gulled, my feet in surf,
naked on the breakwater
    and the huff
    and the puff
and hurl of what is endless
    spitting me salty where it broke —
    I thought of a great laughter.

I thought of laughter enough to sere,
    take, and be forever
done with the naked ego
    in the fever
    and heave
and hoot of what mocks all
    mankind.   I thought of the high queer
    cackle, and spill, and blow

of the drunken self, in time and taken,
    drugged, naked on stone
in the terra cotta summer,
    stripped to bone,
    and honed,

and thrown to the merciless,
   mindless, timeless, unspoken
   lift, beat, break, simmer
and over and over and over and over
   dead, and murdering —
oh, my love! — manless
   and wearing
   and tearing
and strewn presence of all
   I ever dreamed of never
   leaving your safest kiss —

and there I said my joy and was a man.

A Sleep (by Rousseau)

The deer stand black by water, the Lion's head
    comes golden from its cave, the snake goes down
like a brook through ferns.   A man who may be dead
    lies face up in the puddle of the moon.

Night is the dream about him.   Burning birds
    brush at the breasts of cloud, their colors gone
to black and gold.   The trees come down like herds
    to drink beside his sleep.   Later the lion

sniffs him and leaves, the deer go trembling by,
    the snake spills past.   Out of a cloud, Orion
opens and closes on a chalky sky.
    The trees fall back and back into the dawn.

Food Notes

Asparagus is back in all its glory.
Cut on the bias to two inch lengths, quick fried
(with salt) in a wok by Amy Nugatory,
then parboiled (still in the wok) then set aside
(or on low-low) and covered till the steam
of art and mystery have fulfilled the dream

God sent to Amy of his green thumb plumbing
the stirred and watered day of his first making
to steaming essence.   Such is the told coming
of the glory of asparagus.   She, partaking,
gives forth the glory.   The first ecstasies
of sybils tranced in visions, prophecies,

and exhaltations of soul-swelling praise
exult from Amy's rapture and God-gloss.
I, too, taste.   Hm, not bad.   I raise
an almost good chablis by Wendy Bros.
and drink to the body and blood of holy prose.
And glory is something, Heaven knows.

And the glory follows.   Driving, the windows down,
where Newburgh spills untreated essence
into God's Hudson, I sniff.   One waft makes known
it is the promised season.   Pure, intense,
as the soured manger hay breathed forth His story,
asparagus is here in all its glory.

This Morning

This morning in installment property
I rose at five, shaved, showered,
had orange juice, decaffeinated coffee,
and dry toast.   When the cat meowered
I opened a can of hashed guts and fed it.
When the *Times* arrived in a cellophane bag I read it

more or less glancingly to no conclusion,
folded it back in order for my wife,
rinsed the breakfast things in some illusion
that there is a proper order to a life,
and sat to the sunrise in the breakfast nook
with a stack of monthly statements and the check book.

By seven I was paid up.   Had an angel come,
he (he? she? it?) would have found me blameless,
still slightly scented, and precisely at home
with the lawn maintenance men at work in the green seamless
vista and to the well-kept property line
to the unannounced angel.   Till, at half-past nine

my wife comes down.   I pour her coffee and juice
and explain the checks are written and ready to mail.
She turns time's pages.   There can be no excuse
for ignoring the details of how badly we fail.
Having finished she says, "What will you do today?"

and I do not flee the question but turn away.
I go to my desk and arrange clean paper, pen,
neatly next to nothing whatever.   Well,
there's the crossword puzzle.   But I finish at ten,
and still no angel.   There is the mailman's bell:
perhaps he will bring me word.   But I sort through
his strew of announcements, and back to nothing to do.

Christmas Alone In Key West

That Christmas alone in no difference really
in the sun I needed, I strolled by the tree
and picked a star-fruit, but it was dry, mealy,
and puckered the tongue.   Nothing is free.
Certainly not freedom.   Selkirk, demented,
insisted on being left.   He, of course, repented

when the ship was making ready to haul anchor.
He begged to change his mind, but captain and crew
had bloody well had enough of his cantanker.
Some ship would water there in a year or two;
or if not two, five, and if not five, ten.
And maybe his manners would have improved by then.

Mine have already.   Yes I could take a plane
and dodder kindly, while everyone is busy
wrapping and running around and wrapping again
while I sit stranded in bliss watching TV
or I can watch it here without catching a cold.
The barest desert island is growing old.

And that one you have to take whenever you go,
with nothing to do and nothing to retell.
I'm not inclined to wait around for DeFoe
to pretty up the story.   He spins it well
but Crusoe is marzipan.   What I have to say
is there's no reason to go and less to stay.

An Old Man Confesses

I have no cause, and God has not confessed
what purpose time serves.   I am bored by death.
I have its cave-damp glowing in my chest.
I have its stone-dust muddied on my breath.

Carrion.   Age is carrion.   I disgust
even the flesh I am.   And where's the priest
so clean of bloat, so justified and just
he could strip back such skins and find a feast?

Get him away, half-woman as he is
and smelling of old cupboards.   I am gone
into a mud deeper than the abyss
down which his adolescent angels shone

like energies.   Ah, what a world that was!
I could have leaped to Heaven on my own legs!
Now bats hang from the rafters of the house
and blow-flies bore my flaps to lay their eggs.

Only my tongue stays fast.   Rattle and clatter.
As if it signified to say and say.
Maybe saying it is the heart of the matter.
Or just that it costs so little to prattle away.

Say the old fool went prattling to the end.
All words taste better than the gas I sigh.
And while words last me, I can still pretend
that I may phrase some reason not to die.

I doubt it.   Let these words do: "The old sot
lay at his last gasp in a rotten hide
and ran words like a leakage, till the rot
inside the fact had drained.   And then he died."

An Elegy For
Moral Self-Assurance
and Country Virtue

I could have plowed the slim forty and back eighty,
had I been taught, and sweaty proud come in
to strip on the well-rock while Katie,
happily scrubbing my back, turned woman,
delaying supper, since she, too, had to wash,
while I slopped the sow and gave the layers mash.

I could have learned to like it, I suppose,
and to teach the kids their likewise aforesaid.
We'd have had to be careful about shucking our clothes
once they popped in, but we still could whisper in bed.
I could have stood a man on my own land.
There's legend for it.   I think I understand

What the gaffers are saying forever and again,
watching haircuts at Roy's starting at seven
till the last head's done.   It has been made plain.
The good life has grass roots.   I guess I could even
have walked old Betsy wide and staked a spread
and gone to Jesus in a mail-order bed,

honored the community, decently planted
by my professional sons mouthing a hymn,
their Avis doors ajar for the enchanted
airport to better mousetraps, with the slim
forty and back eighty, the whole spread,
on shares to Jimmy Lee Shaw and his boy Fred.

The Logician's Nocturne

The fundamental characteristic of matter
is its existence.   Nothing can exist
apart from its particular properties.
Properties, in existing, interact.
In interaction, particles form cells.
Already creatures, these particular cells
colonize their properties and evolve
to a reflexive cognition.   Reflexive cognition
characteristically recognizes matter
in the forms of what perceives it.   So perceived,
we are the assumptions of our means of perception
insistently reflecting our reflexes.
And why strain to see through them?   At such ease
as creatures shape to in their shaping nests,
I tend the environment of your undressing
to rondures from whose eloquences I learn
reason is prattle till you come to bed.

Loving You Is Something to Do

Imagine having forever nowhere to go.
Or having all the tickets to everywhere
with no good reason for either going or staying.

Isn't that how to be dead in no easy lessons?
Loving you — do you see? — is something to do.
It makes everything else an inactivity.

Time on my hands is dead weight.   It slips through,
and I am left emptied by another death,
until you smile and make me busy being.

Call It a Day

On a day I long since started
to remember from my death
(which may be forgetful),
we drove to Vermont, the kids
a back-seat nest of shrills,
or shouting cow-counts, Judith
a pearl-flesh glow beside me.
We stopped for every ice-cream
and, on Bread Loaf mountain,
at the Homer Noble Farm
with schnauzers, horses,
flowers to the end of the world,
and Robert Frost signing their books
"from a friend."   And after dinner
with him and with Ted and Kay,
on the long lane back to the road

to our house, just at sunset,
Benn said, "Oh, look!"
and there stood a doe in the rut,
as nervous-still as dapple,
and we sat and watched,
and it stood and quivered,
then disappeared.   And we drove
across the shadow of everything,
carried stuff into the house,
started a fire, and Jonnel said
from a face fire-dappled as our doe,
"What an all-over day!"   And Myra:
"I am going to remember everything
forever."   And Judith smiled.
And I did.   And we started to.

Lines for Myra to Grow to

A line drawn straight from my heart to your heart
where you lie sleeping and I sit idle from you
would pass from tissue to a rubber kitten,
on through an oilskin dog, into the wall,
the dry pauses of plaster, then out through my bureau
just missing the .38 among the socks
in their turn-back rolls, like buns, then over the bed,
through the O.E.D., on through another wall,
and back to tissue again.
                        There is no moral
but to place objects in their true disjunction.
—But see, I have said "true."—So there is a moral.

Carving the Turkey

Meleager, one of Jason's heroes, died
in an average hero-storm of blood and guts.
His sisters, being abnormally raucous, cried
so loud so long Apollo changed the sluts
into guinea hens.   *Pot-rak!*   In that death of song
even the name of what they became went wrong.

Meleagris gallopavo ought to have meant
"Meleager's peacock," which will hardly do
for guinea fowl, and which, in bastard descent,
came down to the turkey, though no one, to start with, knew
it was going to be discovered in a place
called Massachusetts.   Once you start to chase

hysteria round itself, what have you got
but that bird that squawks around in ever-decreasing
concentric circles to vanish into its butt
with a sound like *pot-rak?*   Do not look for reason
in the language-gnomes who in *hystera*, the womb
found the organ of *hysteria*.   This Tom

is the misnamed loser at everyone else's feast.
It was Carolus Linnaeus, I think, who chose
his slant and noisy name.   The bird at least
keeps a glazed silence from crop to pope's nose.
So peace and plenty may come even from din
if only by error.   Is everyone served?—Dig in.

Mayflies

Take mayflies, their one-day
blizzard of themselves
up from river mud.

I've seen them,
in less than an hour,
grease three blocks

of Hannibal, Missouri
impassable down hill
from dry Main Street.

We drove to the station
to pick up sister Lu
and couldn't drive up again

over that three inch
green slick of death
fallen from its own wind.

Under the red Schlitz sign
in the cafe window
across the street

they piled a three foot drift.
When we thought
to go there and wait

there was no walking
on the life-slime
our feet crushed.

We couldn't breathe
without inhaling
their excited dying.

We went back
to the summer waiting room
and watched it snow

till a road grader
scraped uphill
and a truck sanded

just barely enough.
Uphill again, Main St.
was any Friday.

To our left
and below, the river
was only misty

behind the stores
that went on selling
everything the same.

And when we had bought
some of it, we drove
back to the farm.

One Betty — Five Skulls

—Saipan, 1944
(A Betty was a Japanese twin-engine bomber)

The search lights caught your enemy and mine.
Balboa's ocean lit with tracer's dawn.
Guns yammered and the falling surf returned
A moment's sound through gunfire and was gone.

Clocks counted, and from sand-bagged coral holes
We were the clocks, and all the sky was lit.
A single eastern star not in the east
Hovered and plunged, and our cheers followed it.

It fell to its own furnace, broke, and blew.
A mountain lit, and flame reached back to fly.
A moment only.   Then the surf renewed
And searchlights cracked and splintered from the sky.

Fast as our cheers we trampled down the night
Racing to find the blackened plow of soil,
Where scattered in the tinfoil ruin of parts
Metal and flesh smoked in a strew of oil.

Perfectly by Orion and The Cross
The mountain darkened and the flesh burned down.
The night healed, sirens beckoned us alive
And on the hills the warning lights came on.

No angers met, no flesh touched flesh and cursed,
Drew blood, reeled back, and had its hatred learned.
But in a solitude of stars, our enemy
Turned down a wheel of dials, and fell, and burned.

Return

—Saipan, 1944

Once more the searchlights beckon from the night
The homing drone of bombers.   One by one
They strike like neon down the plastic dome
Of darkness palaced on our sea and sight
Where avenues of light flower on a stone
To bring the theorem and its thunder home.

Wheels touch and snub, and on the wing's decline
From air and motion into mass and weight
Grace falls from metal like a dancer's glove
Dropped from the hand.   She pauses for the sign
Of one more colored light, and home and late
Crosses to darkness like an end of love.

Under the celebration of the sky
Still calling home the living to their pause
The hatches spill the lucky and returned
Onto the solid stone of not-to-die
And see their eyes are lenses and they house
Reel after reel of how a city burned.

Visibility Zero

—Saipan, 1944

All day with mist against the hurdling wind
The lights hung dressed in halves and a blur.
Air that was solid on a hurtling wing
Hangs sodden, and the parked planes wear like fur
Their look of waiting in the liquid pause
Of cloud descended, in a veil of gauze
The three complete and only trees incite
Their separate loss into the early night.

Fixed to the gauge that swears we cannot see,
Our engines, blind as junk, await the light.
Cards, dice, and spinning coins turn noisily
Into the separate corners of the night.
This was the day we saw our lives made safe,
The day no engines burned and no one gave
A morning thought to chance, but late in bed
Praised the tiered fog that nowhere touched the dead.

Complete in pause, we woke into no need,

Turned back to sleep, stayed dry, and wished for mail.
Ate, and addressed a holiday — a nod
To cancelled schedules, and a word to tell
Our postponed fear that it was not our choice.
And then, released, the barracks lounging voice
In praise of hours where instruments agree
We need not waken and we need not see.

Mr. & Mrs.

It came bone-time.   The metric of ten thousand
alarm clocks striking them from sleep
brought them a tired end from love.   A brook of mist
poured from a steaming spring.   Crows tore open
the stiff film of the sky.   Pines and the stumps of pine
watched them from ages they had forgotten.   The grass
was full of entrances to be avoided.

They sat stiffly and said little.   Strolled sometimes
as far as the road and back but their feet maundered.
They limped back to the porch chairs and sat again.
Everything shook when they touched it.   They learned
to touch little and to be reminded of less.
It was sure soon and no matter.   Their dread was only
which would be first, and each prayed for himself.

SAINTHOOD

She had used one of my textbooks at Bryn Mawr.
    And had canonized me.   Anything, I guess, does
As saint enough when that's what you're looking for.
    But how does one say Om through the tinkle and buzz
Of Freddy's end-of-the-season cocktail bash
For everyone plus the thirty or so who crash?

You wrote the book because you were short of cash
    And were being sued by Jennings, Cole, & Suss.
That isn't reason enough for writing trash
    Not even for sermons.   But that's how it was
you happened to write a text used at Bryn Mawr.
What you managed to write, and what you wrote it for

Don't have to be the same.   They seldom are.
    Except for poems.   And then St. Francis's
Instruction to his shoeless is, "Say *baa*,
    My little sheep.   Not all the Pius's
On Peter's Mountain, shimmering in the flash
Of the given bolts whose lances etch and smash

had more to say, nor cause to say it for.
On earth at Freddy's, in heaven at Bryn Mawr."

The Hero

He died later.   But first his horse shied
and threw him off a mountain.   He grabbed grass,
shrubbery, and then gravel down all the side
of a slope that grows longer as the days pass
and the telling grows steeper; the avalanche he rode,
more thunderous.   All episode,
if told at all, marries its telling and begets
three-headed children.   Today he falls
farther, faster than yesterday.   The sun rises and sets
and he is still rolling.   When (at last) he crawls
out of the talus tomorrow, lakes will have been
buried, whole river systems diverted, the scene
altered through two counties, three.

In the end, however, he will always rise,
look for his hat and find it, brush off one knee
and then the other, slap the dust from his thighs,
climb back to his horse, and, muttering under his breath,
mount, and ride off to his ever greater death.

Statement

Our fathers, whose art was Heaven,
honored be your names.   Our kinship shown,
your need be known on earth
as it were in Heaven.   Show us this way
our doubtful breed, and forgive us
our truth's passing as we forgive those
whose truths pass against us.
And example us from evil.
For yours is the kindling, and the pyre, and storied
endeavor.
               —A man.

The Illusionist

"Watch closely," he said, palming the word "God"
then opening both hands empty, then reaching
to snatch it from the air with a sword through it
and turning that over to show it changed to "History"
which he dropped into his hat, "Now," he said,
picking up a wand, "What will you have back?"
"Justice," I said, improvising.   He tapped
and skulls began brimming over to roll on the stage.
"Aspiration," I said.   He tapped more skulls.
"No," I cried.   "Love!"   He tapped and still they came.
"Purpose!"   He tapped.   "Loyalty!"   He tapped.
"Identity!"   And every tap the dead came grinning.
I understood — was it part of the illusion?—
that these were all who had killed one another
for high cause, "Who'd have killed in any case."
the illusion said, "but killed more comfortably
once they had installed reasons for their motives."
"Reason, then!" I cried.   He put the hat on,
telescoped the wand which he put in his pocket,
and waved the skulls to gas, which vapored leaving
a bare and curtainless stage, and he gone with it.

The Rite

I wrote the president
a letter never sent
of which he took no note.
So in the booth today
I stood alone to pray
as if I had a vote.
As if the government
keeping the covenant
would count it and rejoice
that one man kept the law
and, bowed in holy awe,
surrendered to no choice.
Arrayed like candle flames
the levers with no names
glowed there under my thumb.
I pondered yes and no
the same, then turned to go
with no viaticum.

Remote Control

Along the reef in a last mineral light
a million-silvered school stirs round the diver
like a single curtain turning dark and bright
and dark and bright again, a particular quiver
precisely nervous to some coordinate law
that dwarfs my three dimensions.   Dante saw

saints perform in Heaven, their every motion
computed from God-central.   At M.I.T.
mathematicians puzzling out a notion
screen dancing particles by telemetry
for pieces of a star.   But this is whole
as Dante imagines Heaven, itself its goal.

Numbers, numerology, and fact.
I am no diver and will never be.
And yet the reef becomes my usufruct
by the stunted miracle that made TV.
I click it off to sleep, and every waft
Through moony curtains sends me dreaming daft.

A Gray Spring Morning

I can just see from the attic window
how the jay in the dripping hemlock
rises from her nest
to shake off the weather,
then settles back upon her eggs
the tropic of her breast.

How many small lives there are
at a roof edge!   In the pin oak
a gray squirrel nibbles the buds
that were not there yesterday.
A grackle one branch away
sits by, looking and not looking.
Wary, but sure of himself.

The hemlock is nearly solid
against the sky.   The pin oak,
barely open, barely traces itself
against the total gray.

Below me, under the pin oak, lilac
raises a green cloudhead,
wet and abundant.

Under the lilac,
in red and yellow rain-hats,
children raise their faces
and shake rain
into their laughter.

If God is leaning
from any sill of Heaven
he could ring himself a praise
to out-echo all arches
by looking here.

Last Rites

A jay slants into a dogwood cloud, then out,
a dart through the many-tiered banks of blossoming light.
I invite it and the sun to my funeral
to be my last thoughts down as I mean to think them,
now for then, at these stations of the air.

JOHN CIARDI
UMKC Archives.

Stations of the Air provides 33 poems left among the papers of John Ciardi. They offer us a last breath of genius from one of the great literary men of our time. They demonstrate the wit, skill, profundity, intensity and multiplicity of a great poet and supreme translator—a man for whom art was devotion without pretension, who believed in the life-size but who expected poets and readers to stretch their intellects and emotions. John Ciardi's work did not weaken, but continues to enrich the lives of alert readers who care about depth of engagement and subtlety of interpretation.

MICHAEL BERGT is represented by John Pence Galleries in San Francisco and Midtown Payson Galleries in New York City, as well as other galleries nationwide. He has collaborated on many art/literary projects.

MICHAEL ANNIS and DAVID ASHLEY often collaborate in the book arts. ANNIS has designed for BkMk Press since 1986. He is the originator and editor of Howling Dog Press and *Stiletto*. ASHLEY, a professional calligrapher, is also a hand bookbinder, illustrator, designer and poet.

BkMk Press wishes to give special thanks to the following members of the class of '41, University of Kansas City, for help in funding this book:

Claire (Seward) Hildebrand
Barbara Jean (Warner) Higgins
Betty (Silcott) Hough
William B. Elic
Rev. and Mrs. Arleigh W. Lassiter
Marjorie (Lovejoy) Williams
Thomas D. Pickell, Sr.
Winifred (Woods) Perry
Beverly (Nixon) Smith
Edward and Mary Ellen Olsson
Bernice (Ross) Peters
George W. Biltz
Bernice (Wisemore) Delmont

The University of Missouri-Kansas City Office of Advancement provided special assistance in making this book possible.

The University of Missouri-Kansas City Archives provided the photo of John Ciardi. Photo by Michael Mardikes.